Just The Way it is

By Megan Morales

Illustrated By:
Gabriel Uji Rodriguez

Copyright © 2014 by Megan Morales.

Library of Congress Control Number: 2014959408

Illustrated by: Uji Rodriguez.

All rights reserved.
This book or any portion thereof may
not be reproduced or used in any manner
whatsoever without the express written
permission of the publisher except for
the use of brief quotations in a book review.

Printed in the United States of America
First Printing, Hardcover Edition December 2013

ISBN-13: 978-1-940812-77-9
ISBN-10: 1940812771

Tari Books
PO Box 56
Albertville, Alabama 35950

www.pdmipublishing.com

Dedication

I would like to dedicate this story to the children who have Epilepsy, and are trying to find themselves in this world. And, the children who want to learn about it.

Acknowledgement

I never thought one of my stories would be published, because I thought I was too young or because I thought it just sucked in general, no matter how hard I worked on it. But, this story held something near and dear to my heart. It was about something that was part of me, and I never gave up on it.

I would like to thank my mom and dad, who kept pushing and pushing me not to give up on it, despite the rejections I received. I would also like to thank my family, (especially my cousin Gabriel Uji Rodriguez for the illustrations for this story). And my Facebook family for also urging me to continue.

I would also like to thank (personally) Vance Major. I wouldn't have gotten this far without him, and I truly appreciate that.

Just The Way it Is

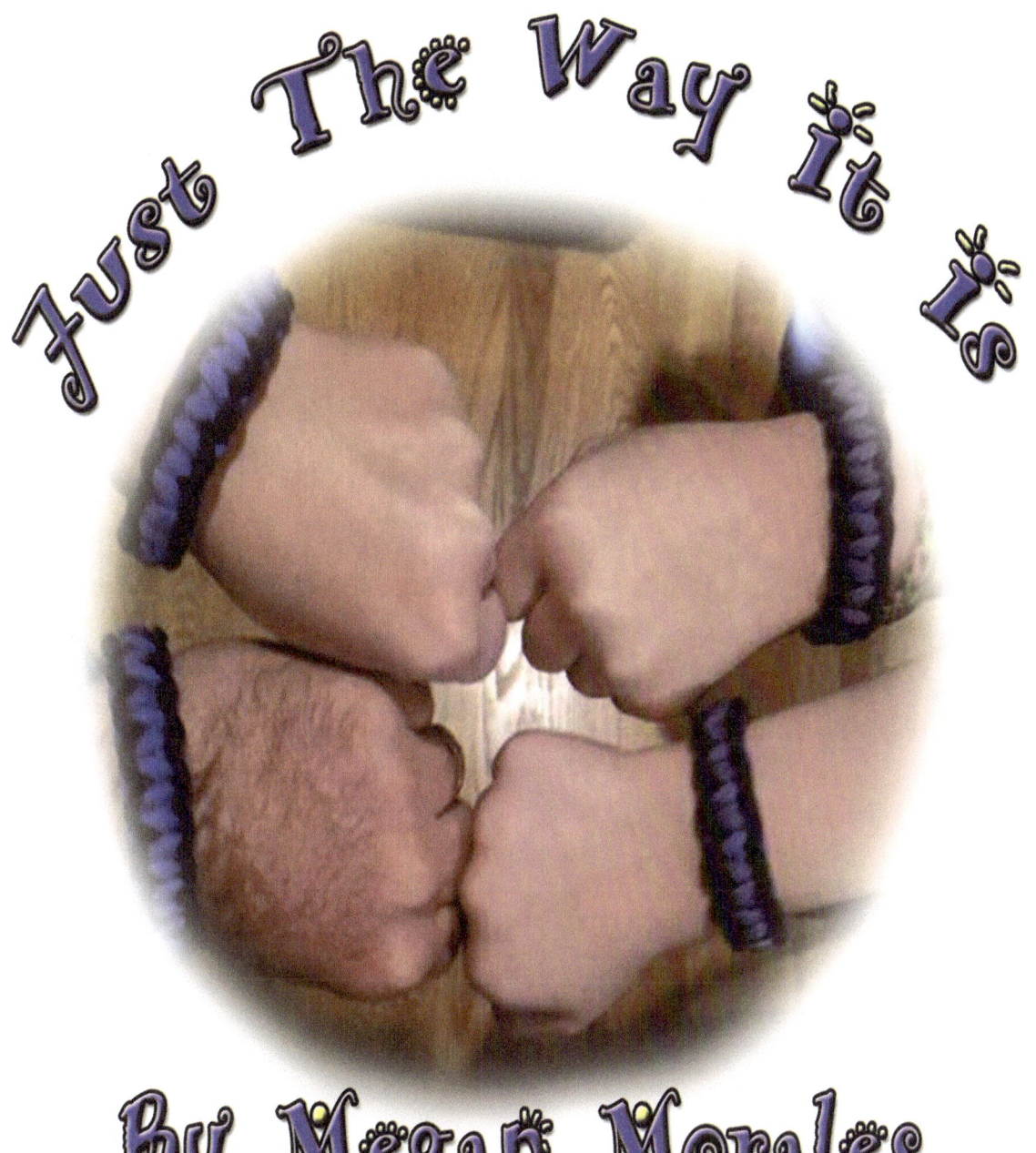

By Megan Morales

Help Support Epilepsy Awareness

Gather around my dear children, gather and see!

What a wonderful thing avoiding epilepsy stigma can be!

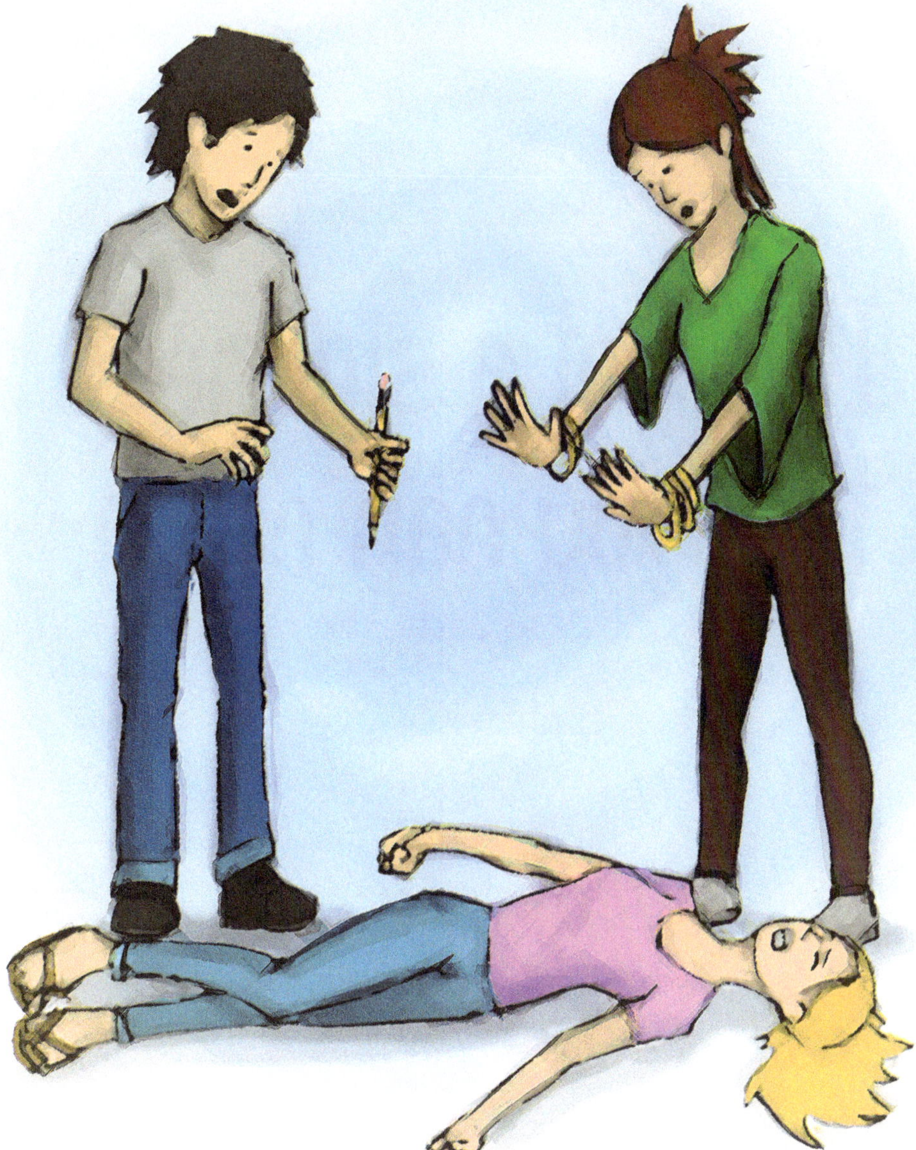

It is not a sickness
that you can catch;

It's not passed
on by touch--

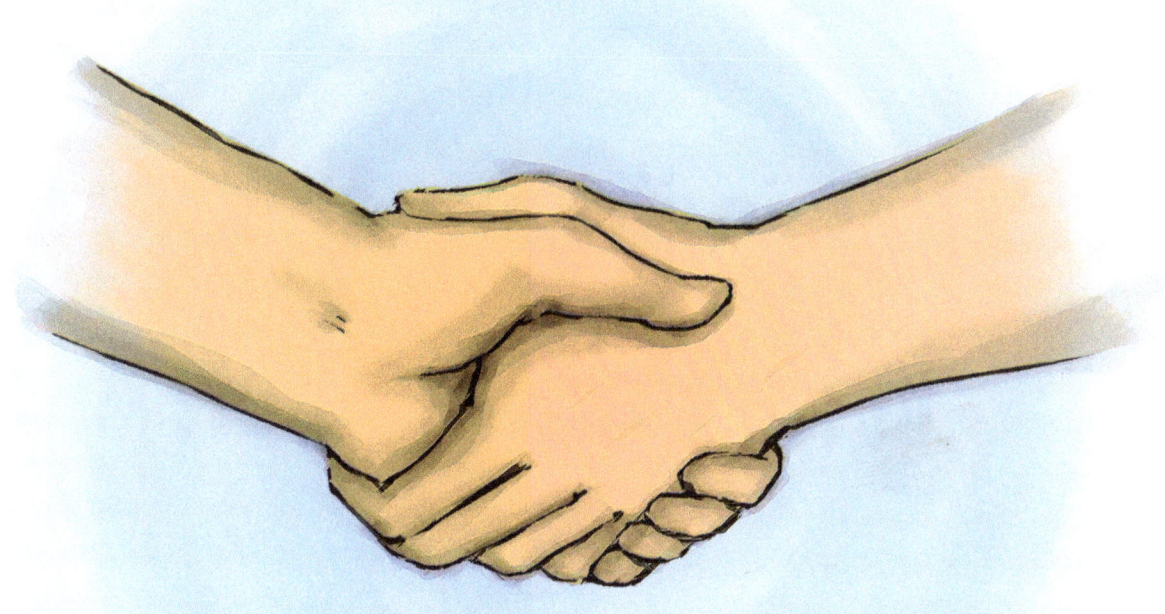

Nor is it something
to be ashamed of,

So perish the thought!

So please my dear children,
try to remember,

That everyone has a heart,

And they can be quite tender.

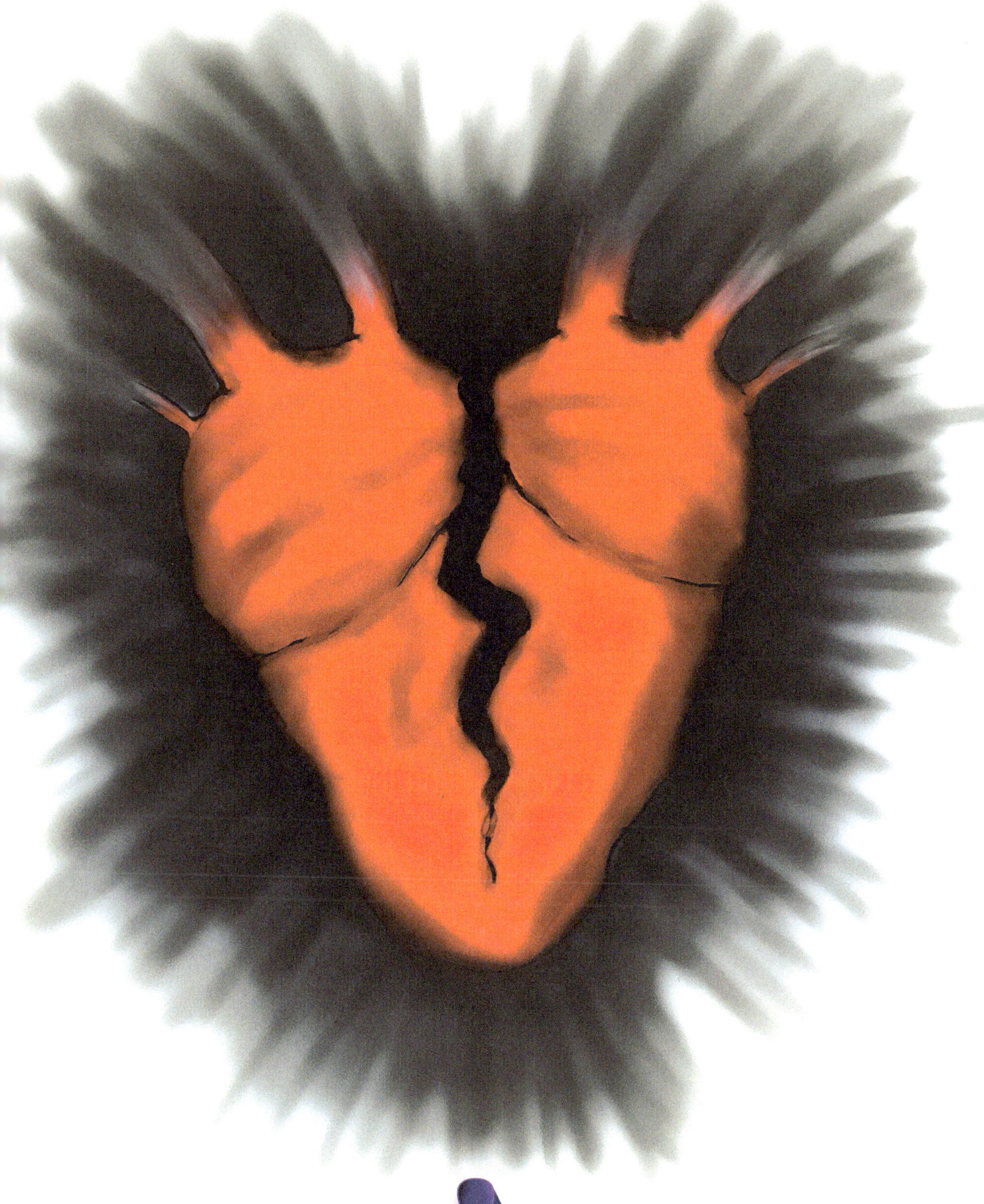

Just remember that we have more energy in our minds;

We feel a lot of things like sparks flying by,

and then, the energetic parts of our brains go wonky,

as if they were circuits, temporarily unplugged,

but then, the moment passes, and we are fine.

People fear what they don't understand,

and we don't understand them at times,

but that doesn't mean we have demons inside.

We cannot stop the seizures;

those sudden bouncing lightning-bolts that go off in our minds--

We feel sad, but we don't let the feeling overcome us.

So please don't make fun,

If you find out about our illness,

Because it's really not helpful,

And makes us feel quite dreadful.

Don't push us away because you don't understand;

accept us,

just once,

and reach out your hand.

Type of Seizures

(General)

- GRAND MALS (Generalized Tonic-Clonic). Person loses consciousness, have convulsions small or big, and their muscles lock up.

- ABSENCE SEIZURES are when a person stares off into space, and loses brief consciousness.

- MYOCLONIC SEIZURES are jerking movements that happen once in a while.

- CLONIC SEIZURES are consistent jerking movements that happen over and over again.

- TONIC SEIZURES make a person stiffen up.

- ATONIC SEIZURES cause loss of muscle tone.

(SIMPLE)

- SIMPLE MOTOR SEIZURES are a jerking, muscle rigidity spasm seizure.

- SIMPLE SENSORY SEIZURES are unusual sensations affecting either the vision, hearing, smell, taste, or touch.

- SIMPLE PSYCHOLOGICAL SEIZURES are disturbances of memory or motions.

- COMPLEX SEIZURES involve lip smacking, chewing, fidgeting, walking or other repetitive movements.

- PARTIAL SEIZURE WITH SECONDARY GENERALIZATION is a type of seizure with symptoms that are initially associated with a preservation of consciousness that then evolves into a loss of consciousness and convulsions.

The Do's and Don'ts of Epilepsy.

DON'T

- Don't put anything in someone's mouth if they are having a seizure, because they can harm themselves and you in the process.

- Don't restrain them.

- Don't call 911 if they have epilepsy or any kind of seizure disorder, unless the seizure lasts over 5 minutes.

- Don't interfere.

- Don't move the person.

- Don't panic.

- Don't crowd the person.

DO

- Do remove any objects around the person that they may hurt themselves with.

- Do loosen tight clothing.

- Do put them on their side in case they vomit.

- Do make them comfortable after a seizure.

- Do call your doctor to inform them what happened.

- Do look for medical ID. (A bracelet or a necklace)

- Do talk to them in soothing/reassuring tones.

Disneyland Epilepsy Awareness Day Information

It's in Anaheim California, on November 6th every year.
People of all ages with Epilepsy can come with their family and friends.
And people whose lives have been touched by Epilepsy.
Or people who want to raise awareness.

The link to buy tickets & to buy a bag that's full of prizes is:
http://epilepsyawarenessday.org/event-information.html

BRACELETS FOR EPILEPSY AWARENESS BY MEGAN MORALES

They are eight dollars, with free shipping, unless its ordered from the UK.

Then you will have to pay $2.50 for the shipping..

Instructions on how to measure your wrist.

You put a string around your wrist comfortably, and measure the string to that point.

*Order form on following page

PDMI Publishing, LLC
P.O Box 56
Albertville, Alabama 35950

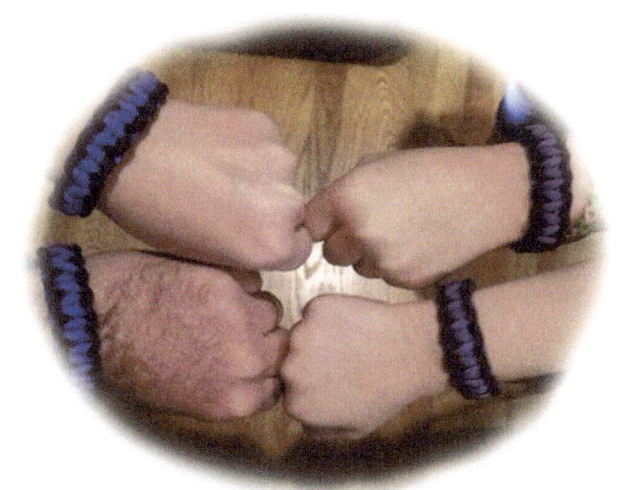

Bracelets are $8 with free shipping if shipped in the US

Please add 2.50 for shipping and handling for all orders outside the US

No cash, stamps or CODs

Must be paid in U.S. Dollars. Prices subject to change.

Payment must accompany all orders.

Name: _____

Address: _____

City: _____ State: _____ Zip: _____

Email: _____

I have enclosed $_____ for _____ Bracelets

CPSIA information can be obtained at www.ICGtesting.com
Printed in the USA
BVOW10s0612210415

397027BV00001B/1/P